How to...

"Set up a Family Budget"

"A budget tells us what we can't afford, but it doesn't keep us from buying it."

William Feather

TABLE OF CONTENTS

"Modern man drives a mortgaged car over a bond-financed highway on credit-card gas."

Earl Wilson

INTRODUCTION

"The average family exists only on paper and its average budget is a fiction, invented by statisticians for the convenience of statisticians."

Sylvia Porter

Unlike the quote provided above, seemingly reflective of general opinion on family budgets today, we will attempt to take a much more **positive approach to budgeting, as a family oriented, user-friendly, financial management and planning tool and life-enabler.**

However, when reflecting on family budgeting and inquiring as to why not more families are actually using it, it becomes self-evident that similar skepticism runs rampant and deep in reality and society, even globally so.

Once you start probing family budgets, expending time and energy researching the subject in-depth, it becomes quite clear, that most families are caught in a vicious, almost never-ending cycle of *"What comes in must go out."*

Most families might feel that budgeting is a futile effort, unnecessarily burdening them with thoughts and ways, to go broke methodically and slowly, without the creature comforts and indulgences of our human modern-day society.

Others might voice that they feel as if they are merely throwing money away, in a never-ending and dizzying spiral of spend, spend, spend. People are getting deeper and deeper into debt, no matter how hard they try to get out of it. Questions are then raised : How do we stop these courses of action? How do we change the thinking around family fiscal discipline?

Put simply, in "How to set up a Family Budget", we focus in on how to empower families to set up better, more realistic budgets, stick to them and celebrate their successes (and learn from their failures!)

Families eventually do have a monthly surplus, see their savings start to grow, consolidate their debt, set aside discretionary funds and personal allowances, build their wealth and become more aware of their pro-active involvement and responsibility regarding their lives and finances. This is when excitement builds and fundamental thought patters as well as spending attitudes are changed.

Budgeting is seen as an accurate measurement of success when significant behavioral transformation is taking place on the landscape of the family budget, spending habits and financial patterns we observe over time!

Do you ever feel that you do not have enough cash at the end of the month to pay bills, buy necessities of life? Are you barely making a dent in your credit card debt balance, no matter how hard you try?

Here is a reality check for all of us: if we choose to spend it, it is gone for good. We cannot spend it on anything else. Are you perhaps worried about a nest egg for your golden years or savings for early retirement? Then you have arrived at a source that can provide some prudent tips on how to start, finish, implement, stick to, revise and refine a family budget.

The family budget is a dynamic process, even more so than a mere static work-product, result, process-outcome or document. It will, can and should change over time. It becomes a barometer of a family's fiscal circumstance, resources and health.

Maybe budgeting is not as much about reflecting on what you cannot have, but more about thoughts on how to stretch, invest and spend your earned dollars more wisely. In short, it is about making your money going further.

This quick-reference how-to guide was developed to assist you with setting up your own personal, household and family budget, to help you with all of the above and more!

A couple of general money-savings will also be provided in these pages. There are also thoughts and spending patterns that need to change, in order to become fiscally more disciplined and many techniques, attitudes, habitual behaviors that we need to un-earth, evaluate and possibly change, before you even start budgeting.

For example, being a bargain hunter looking for good buys, cutting down on careless spending, being on the lookout for careless credit card spending and letting the person who handles money best in your household actually take care of it, are all good examples of what we mean.

For most households, a budget is no more than a spending plan. Any spending plan can help you see where your money is going. It fits your spending to your income. It reflects how we get the things we want and need most, while being ready and prepared for bills we must pay every month.

For most families it is simply about making a budget you can live with and stick to easily. It is not a difficult exercise, but one most people fear, avoid or dread because of the unknown and perceived complexity of it (sometimes wrongfully so!).

Part of the goal of this guide is to demystify family budgeting and highlight an easy systematic process to setting up a quality family budget.

Many things actually drive our expenditure. We choose to spend our money on things we value, need, prefer or consciously choose. For some it is clothes, for others it might be something as simple as taking that yearly vacation.

Whether you are making financial decisions for yourself or your household, you might have to make some serious choices and adjustments regarding your financial freedom and situation.

"How to Set up a Family Budget", is a quick-reference, easy, how-to guide, meant to take you through the typical, who, why, when, what, where and how questions typically asked when considering fiscal planning for the household and or budgeting in general for your family need, means and circumstance, now and for the future.

Budgeting is not just about restricting spending and living a cheapskate life. It is about insights, wisdom, informed decisions, action and sustained discipline when it comes to your household financials.

This guide will invite you to learn more in these pages about systematic budgeting. It focuses on practical application and zooms in to apply these "best practice suggestions" in your own home. It empowers you to put together a dynamic, financial plan that suits your pocketbook, means and circumstance.

Financially speaking, assess quickly where you think you and your family are today.

- What kind of a picture do you have?
- Could you come up with something?
- Did you have the data and numbers you needed?
- Would you be able to plan for where you want to be and start living your life today as a fiscally sound and disciplined family with the information you have at your disposal at present?

Money makes the world go round! It is no secret that some of us have more, some have less. We deal with our own personal finances and cash management distinctly differently. Households have varying needs, means and circumstance. Our money-management skills are also at different levels, as is our debt and savings!

Budgeting has to do with most of these perspectives and reflections.

The purpose and goal of family budgeting is:

- financial situational analysis and informed awareness,
- (ii) cutting cost,
- (iii) gaining control or curbing spending <u>and</u>
- (iv) Starting to save, building up wealth and liquid assets over time.

There are many phases and steps to go through when creating a budget.

If you are looking for ways to manage your money better, making it reach and stretch further, and providing you with financial security and a more solid future, then you have come to the right place.

In this brief introduction on family budgets, we have already introduced our first couple of key questions

- Why an e-book or how-to guide on setting up a family budget?
- Why would or do you need a family budget?
- What is the business case for and rationale behind family budgeting?

- What are the benefits and advantages of a family budget?

We elaborate a little more below. For most people, a family budget is the equivalent of a simplistic process: <u>money is earned and comes in; money is spent and moves out!</u>

It is a fluid, easy-flow, one-directional, cash management process. It is driven by daily life, a spending-orientation, or no plan at all!

For most families, income is also fixed and outflow typically increases over time, as the needs of the family fluctuates and changes. Loading up on debt is also very typical for the majority of our families. If this sounds very much like a vicious circle, it is. Most families are caught up in it and constantly battle to get out.

Mostly, we think that we wisely spend our money on necessities like food and clothing, gas and household or family needs, but can rarely put a finger on where the money actually goes, let alone produce a budget!

A good place to start is to monitor these expenses.

Take stock of your fiscal situation. Start with assessing where exactly you are in your financial life and circumstance. Most of us think we know, but we really do not.

That is, until we take the time to actually list, study and analyze the situation. Figure out what your financial worth is, look at all financial goals, and set a timeline for reaching them. Does this sound like an action plan? Where do you start?

A good suggestion is your bank statements, tax return and recent current credit report – a financial asset statement if you will -and an overview of the current situation.

The premise is simple: you can not get to arrive where you want to be if you do not know where you are today, what it will take to get where you need to be and how to get there.

A well thought out, planned and realistic budget will serve as a roadmap to get you there. It is a financial tool facilitating your financial dreams, goals and aspirations, making them become a reality. Budgeting will enable you to actually reach your financial targets and set goals.

WHAT IS YOUR CURRENT FINANCIAL STATUS?

How do you define financial worth? Is it cash in the bank, savings and checking accounts, RRSP's, stocks and investment portfolio?

Remember, anything you have that is of value counts. All your assets form part of your financial picture and health. Ask yourself: What is your take-home pay, after deductions? How are you paid? Is it monthly, weekly, bi-weekly? Then you need to budget accordingly!

Think about all other sources of income, temporary, seasonal, part-time - extra income, found money and bonuses that you might have.

Maybe deciding to leave it out of your family budget altogether is wise and advisable? (we will delve into this question a little later).

Try to find ways to do without some small creature comforts and pleasures to reap bigger rewards later.

Starting small, early and now, with discipline and commitment, a steady, consistent pace and amount every month, tracking and optimizing financial phenomena like 'compound interest' (which we will describe later), will all feed into this process.

We will take this journey into budgeting together to see how it can change lives: yesterday, today and tomorrow!

Back to listing assets and thinking about savings: consider all banks, savings and loans, credit union accounts, money market accounts, certificates of deposit, Christmas club accounts you might have. ALL LIQUID ASSETS that can be readily turned into cash need to be included.

Consolidate accounts if you have too many accounts spread out and save on banking fees. Improve tracking actual spending better and more easily. Earn higher interest and have less exposure to identity theft or fraud by getting a good handle on your current situation.

For most individuals and families alike, this step is quite a revelation. It forms the basis and baseline for deeper analysis and scrutiny.

Other assets might include things like: art, precious metals, sculptures, paintings, collections, antiques, jewelry and more.

Most of us are used to having a short-term focus on money and budgeting. A paradigm-shift is required to move us towards a more in-depth, longer-range view and planning.

Set short, mid and long term goals, have a definite structured plan, read up on family budgeting, personal financials and fiscal management strategies. All of this will help us focus on what is important for our needs, requirements and circumstance, while keeping financial discipline and budgeting in the forefront of our busy lives.

This is never an easy task amidst all the hustle and bustle that is our daily lives!

Most of the published literature on family budgeting in general centers around how to get out of debt, stay out of debt and live a full and prosperous life.

Some suggest frugal living is the answer and offer 'your money or your life' perspectives, where you cannot necessarily have both. There are many examples advocating the cheapskate monthly makeover that focuses on shaving costs off expenses and living frugally.

Market providers both online and offline, offer various budget kits which offers worksheets and more and there is always the handy tip-like Coles notes and the pocket idiots' guide to living on a budget.

Other sources focus on becoming totally debt free, debt proofing your life, getting a life and choosing simplicity or how to address credit card debt and expenditure.

This 'how to' guide is a little different.

We have chosen to take a very hands-on, practical approach to fiscal management and get you started, walking through the budgeting steps and set you up, sending you off, well and good, on-course to solid budgeting in your family and household!

This brings us to the <u>Who, What, When, Where, Why</u> and <u>How</u> part of the discussion. These form the dynamic, interacting and inter-dependent elements, systems and processes that form "family budgeting."

<u>Who?</u> Every family situation is uniquely different and distinctive. There is no one-size-fits-all answer and solution for everyone.

Some of the tips in this guide might apply to your unique means and circumstance, and others may not have any significant impact or practical application at all.

In general terms, you will find handy ideas, hints, process steps, practical savings suggestions and budgeting that might have gone unnoticed before.

The information provided is general and should be evaluated on an individual and contextualized basis. Remember to consult a financial advisor when making fiscal decisions that could affect the financial health, well-being and future of you and your treasured family.

There are various different families in question here too: single-income, single-parent, blended and/or extended families, double-income households, stay-at-home mothers working part-time from the home to make ends meet, social-supported and/or subsidized families, families at risk, divorced household with shared parenting and financial responsibilities, debt-ridden or bankruptcy families and numerous others. We hope to offer something for everyone.

<u>What?</u> Family budgeting is a structured process and planning activity, dealing with a family's financial resources and context.

This hands-on approach puts expense items into categories as another helpful strategy. This is done to get a better handle on the current situation and offers somewhat of a reality check to most that choose to undertake this journey.

Some of the categories could be:

- Obligations – list each item under headings like: home: mortgage or rent; association fees and professional dues; insurance: health, auto, home, renters' and life; tuition, day care; loans: car loan, student loan, bank fees and interest; taxes, property taxes and so on.

- Necessities – again list each item under headings like : food, groceries, gas, yard maintenance, security, pest control, utilities: gas, water, electric, garbage, sewer; school lunches, household supplies, car maintenance, monthly parking, housekeeper, household repairs, internet service, dry cleaning, cable TV and more.
- Pocket expenses – treat this as a whole category, covering: lunch at work, snacks, sodas, coffee, drinks, parking, tolls, newspapers, magazines, batteries, postage, shipping, mail
- Family Allowances – another whole category including items like : parties, entertainment, weekend outing, movies, concerts, other entertainment and events, home improvements and decorating, magazine and other subscriptions, dining out and fast food, furniture
- Personal allowances - clothing, hobbies, personal recreation, books, CD's, manicures, hair, alterations, shoe repair, personal gifts, luggage, night out with friends, gardening, films, processing, video rentals, sports/recreation, family gifts, contributions, donations, computer software and other related items.

When and Where? In the interest of brevity, we combine the next two facets. Our best assessment to answering when and where the best place and time would be to start a family budget would be to answer unequivocally: HERE AND NOW!

It demands attention as it directly affects our daily lives and well-being. Without delay, hesitation or postponement, we need to step up and protect our family interest, financial health and future.

Accounting brings accountability! A wealth management guru is often quoted as saying. This rings so true. It is hard to ignore, if we are confronted with objective cold hard financial facts that tell us that we are in trouble.

Why budget? Families, as mentioned before, have diverse reasons and motivations for budgeting. Briefly summarized, people budget for a couple of reasons:

- To gain control of their financial life, monthly bills and spending
- Be prepared and avoid surprises
- Save for a major purchase
- Opt out of a vicious circle of ever-spiraling debt or spend-now-pay-later thinking
- Expand their lifestyle(s)
- Retire early

- Eliminate money as a source of tension and topic for argument
- Rediscover that the best things in life are FREE!
- Becoming self-reliant and empowered to know that debt does not rule their lives anymore!

We promise even more on this a little later!

Family Budgets Defined

How to budget? Some general strategies are helpful in assisting families to set up a budget or budget better.

- The first significant step is to <u>change your thinking about money</u>, <u>shift your attitude toward spending</u>, <u>actually focus on saving money</u>, <u>planning ahead</u> and <u>driving for success</u>
- Develop a greater awareness of how you earn, manage, save and spend money
- Awareness of how others would lure, entice and want you to spend your money (advertisers, retailers, and manufacturers)
- To stop participating and playing the "Keeping-up-with-the-Jones's game," living with a false sense of wealth and security, while over-extending your self and financial resources, beyond your means. Do not envy others and lust after things that they might have or even worse, get deeper into debt to compete or keep up appearances. It is counterproductive and can ruin lives!
- Delay purchases – learn and do, sometimes without having to buy!
- Set solid financial and budget goals for yourself and your family that you can work on individually and collectively to achieve together
- Set spending limits and stick to them
- Do not make ends meet utilizing credit cards, stay away from ATM machines, cash, cash advances, do not cheat on your budget
- Understand your income – know where the money is coming from and how it varies throughout a one-year cycle
- Understand your expenses – monthly and irregular, unexpected expenses
- Set a few realistic financial goals

- Know your own habits, spending, temptation, and where the areas of risk and exposure are.
- Set up savings and spending mechanisms that work, reserve and growth accounts and have the right number of credit cards
- Make an income plan – detail is important
- Plan your obligations and must pays – smooth out large size bills with reserve accounts
- Plan your necessities and look for ways to economize
- Set aside pocket money for daily incidentals
- Create a family allowance to cover entertainment
- Create a personal allowance
- Balance and consolidate, wise decisions and trade-offs – agree and stick to it
- Live happily on a budget
- Welcome to frugal living mode! Cutting back on living expenses – alternatives for simple living
- re-examine why you work and how you live
- stop tossing your hard-earned cash away
- shopping, overwork, stress and debt (some refer to this as an illness quipped: 'Affluenza'!)
- celebrate when you have money left over at the end of the month – indulge a little and reward yourself – rewarding patience and persistence! Not just the doing good and sticking with it

'How to set up a Family budget', is advocating a new code of fiscal honor for our families, so to speak. It proposes family budgets, that ask for wisdom (best choices and decisions), discipline (sticking to it), honesty (no cheating), persistence and celebration when we do it right!

THE RATIONALE AND PROCESS OF BUDGETING

Here are twelve good reasons to get you started:

1. Family budgets are used as a baseline, analysis-tool and roadmap. It is a useful tool and guide. It tells you whether you are headed in the direction you want to be headed in financially. It helps you to move from spending to saving and good fiscal balance, management and responsibility.

You may have goals and dreams, but if you do not set up guidelines for reaching them and you do not measure your progress, you may end up going so far in the wrong direction you can never make it back. Can you imagine the government or a major corporation operating without a budget? No, and neither should you.

2. It is often described and justified as an empowering enabler. A budget lets you control your money instead of your money controlling you.

3. A budget is **a realistic estimate and true reflection of current circumstance and means, a type of financial situation-analysis that** will tell you if you are living within your means. Before the widespread use of credit cards, you could tell if you were living within your means because you had money left over after paying all your bills.

There are lots of family budgeting tools available on line that make it a fun and enjoyable task and activity, to assess and analyze your family's financial situation with minimum effort. (www.MoneyPants.com)

There is also lots of free financial software and most of it sets up easily and provides you with a detailed family budget online. It manages your finances, hassle-free and almost effortless.

Well, almost! It will require input and minimum effort through hands-on involvement in setting it up, populating, maintaining and editing it. Mvelopes.com is a good example of market offerings that are available at no cost to you, just waiting for the motivated family budgeter to embrace and try it out!

Some websites offer free financial newsletters by e-mail, with lots of money saving tips, budget advice, and other relevant personal and family-related financial information (www.planabudget.com).

The availability, accessibility, virtual marketplace, ease of use and more of **credit cards** has made the need for family budgets much less obvious. Many people do not even realize they are living far beyond their means until they are knee deep in debt, struggling to make ends meet and sinking fast into murky financial waters.

Budgeting is and can be a life and money saver, a reality check, BUT ALSO a remedy!

4. **A budget can help you meet your savings goals.** It includes a mechanism for setting aside money for savings and investments.

5. **Following a realistic budget frees up spare cash** so you can use your money on the things that really matter to you instead of frittering it away on things you do not even remember buying.

6. A budget **helps your entire family focus on common goals.** It is unifying families in mutual purpose and effort, working together towards a successful outcome and reward.

7. A budget **helps you prepare for emergencies** or **large or unanticipated expenses** that might otherwise knock you for a loop financially.

8. A budget **can improve your marriage**. A good budget is not just a spending plan; it is a communication tool. Done right, a budget can bring the two of you closer together as you identify and work towards common goals and reduce arguments about money.

9. A budget **reveals areas where you are spending too much money,** so you can refocus on your most important goals.

10. A budget can **keep you out of debt or help you get out of debt.**

11. A budget actually **creates extra money for you to do use on things that matter to you.**

12. A budget **helps you sleep better at night** because you do not lie awake worrying about how you are going to make ends meet.

Nevertheless, despite all these wonderful reasons quoted above, people are still hesitant to commit to family budgeting as standard practice in their households. We might again want to probe a little deeper still and ask why?

TOP THREE CAUSES OF BUDGET FAILURE

Many people make an honest attempt to budget, but become discouraged and give up before they are able to accomplish any significant financial gain. The top three causes of budget failure come into play before you even begin to set up your budget. Awareness of these budget busters, is your first line of defense in the Battle of the Budget.

Budget Buster #1 - Negative Attitude

It cannot be emphasized enough--a positive attitude about budgeting is essential to your success. If you think of budgeting in negative terms (such as a financial diet, financial handcuffs, restrictive, penny-pinching, a sacrifice, etc.), you are sure to fail, unless you are a martyr or a masochist who finds some strange reward in a punishing experience. For purposes of this article, we will assume that you are neither.

A positive attitude means you think of a budget as a means to an end--a way to achieve your dreams and goals--and that postponing the instant gratification of spending all the money you earn is worth the rewards you will earn in the end.

Budget Buster #2 - Lack of Motivation

What is your motivation for budgeting? Are you trying to appease a nagging spouse? Following the terms of a debt repayment plan with a consumer credit counseling agency? Complying with an agreement made in bankruptcy court? These are not bad motivations, but they are external pressures and will probably not be easy to maintain over time. The best motivations are internally generated: do you honestly believe that budgeting can help you meet your goals?

If you need a little help in the motivation department, see "Twelve Reasons Budgeting Can Improve Your Life". A quick re-read of these will surely inspire and ignite a motivational spark or two!

Budget Buster # 3 - Unrealistic Expectations

What do you expect to gain from instituting and following a budget? Do you think that setting up a budget will reveal large caches of hidden cash or that the budget fairy will sprinkle fairy dust over your budget and magically transform your spending habits after a month or two of tracking expenses?

The reality is that budgeting is an endurance event--those who stick with it, through thick and thin, will come out ahead financially. Do not expect miracles. What you WILL see if you stick with it is steady, measurable progress towards the goals that really matter to you.

Starting a budget without having a <u>positive attitude</u>, <u>internal motivation</u>, and <u>realistic expectations</u>, will probably set you up for failure. You can greatly increase your chances of success by ruling out the three biggest budget busters before you even begin.

Family budgeting – just the thought of it makes most of us cringe. However, mostly, we do attempt to curb our spending and live within our means. Others fall into bad habits, habitual spending patterns or impulse shopping and over-extend themselves, landing knee-deep in debt!

Ironically, one of the first remedies for any debt consolidation or repair strategy, is to **take a long hard look at the budget and financial patterns within the household! It is almost like running a diagnostic.**

To take a closer look, you are in effect placing your family dollars under a magnifying glass and microscope. This can prove both challenging and painful for most people. We hope to alleviate some of that initial discomfort and apprehension with this handy step-by-step guide and tips.

Most financial advisors will tell you that you have to reward yourself for good fiscal responsibility, discipline and habits, to increase your motivation and success levels.

Budgeting is the first step, sticking with and to it, a close second and the sometimes overlooked but ever-important reward, has to keep the motivation going! To repeat and continue to experience the benefit of the budgeting cycle and discipline could be an uphill battle, but there are calmer seas ahead.

Cash management, savings, planning for retirement, setting financial goals etc. active and hands-on, is becoming increasingly important for the survival and well-being of our families everywhere.

Be your own best expert with coming up with new ideas on how to <u>save money</u>, <u>budget better</u> and <u>spend less</u>! Your unique strategies stem from a deep understanding of your own situation, demands, and needs. Discover which tips and ideas work best for you. After all, fiscal management and finances are definitely not a one-size-fits-all solution environment. It is personal, customized and unique.

In the following section, we will briefly refer back to the family budget defined and look at some of its elements and criteria, purpose and functions.

- What is a family budget?
- What constitutes a good family budget?
- What should it contain and look like?

What is the family budget again? It is a pro-active, hands-on approach, focused, technical and disciplined strategy to getting a handle on the current financial situation in the home and family,

It concerns setting realistic, SMART financial goals for the household, sticking to it, celebrating successes, learning from failures and trying again if you do not succeed or get it right the first time round .It is about shifting focus completely from a mainly spending to a savings orientation. Cash and money-management 101 for everyone!

We have laid out what a family budget is, does and affects. A brief mention of what constitutes as good family budget and the elements that it contains as well as its appearance, format and functional role follows.

All of us have a wish list of new things that we want. There is always things we would find and places to spend our money. Take the time to make a list of these things. Let everyone who shares cost in your home to have input into making and finalizing this list.   Write down what you want most. Beside the goal, write how much it will cost. Split it into goals with ongoing costs and the cost per month, and goals with a one-time cost and list the actual total cost (including all hidden fees, taxes, shipping and or other charges that might apply. Now, next to these columns, start to prioritize these goals.

<u>Which goal comes first?</u> You need to decide which goal on your list <u>should</u> come first. Talk this over with the other members of your family. If you live alone, think it over yourself. Try to list your top four goals and decide what you can fit into your budget.

A 'good' budget is in the eyes of the creator or beholder alike! Some suggested, but by no means comprehensive criteria follows:

- Budget is both process and product
- Collaborative, engaged, hands-on effort
- Characterized by communication and mutual agreement
- It advocates involvement and exchange

- It is real-time and reality-based
- Factual
- Accurate
- A financial check-up and check-in on the family finances, household dollars, situations, behaviors, and resources.
- An action-plan, future-oriented
- Offers a peak into the past, scrutinizes and enlightens the present, while planning and promising a future
- Goal and results oriented

The Family Budget Process

This brings us to the family budget process. We might ask questions like:

- How to set up a family budget?
- How should a family budget be used?

Insights around the tools and techniques of family budgeting could also be useful:

- Practical suggestions for setting up a budget?
- A step-by-step summary of a family budget process
- Hints, tips, tricks and tools for setting up a family budget

Stay tuned for more…

To get us started and in order to set up a monthly budget, follow these five easy steps:

Step one: find out your monthly take-home pay

Step two: find out what your expenses are

Step three: find out how much you spend on each expense

Step four: see if your monthly expenses match monthly take-home pay

Step five: Balance your budget. This means in your family budget you need to ensure that you are spending matches take-home pay. It might indicate that you have to cut back on spending to balance.

It sounds too good to be true and too simplistic. However, in the end, that is all there is to this family budgeting process! Initially at least. Let us look at these steps one at a time.

- **Finding out your monthly take-home pay**

Your income is your pay, after some money is deducted. Think taxes, insurance and Social Security. Answer the following questions:

What is your monthly take-home pay? Do other people share expenses in your home?

As mentioned before, total all of the households' monthly take-home pay. This will include all sources of income for all contributing members of the household.

- **Finding out what your expenses are**

This brings up other pressing questions:

What are your monthly expenses? Where does the money in fact go every month?

Most people are surprised to learn that it may go for things that we do not need at all. Writing your expenditures down provides us with the unique opportunity to visualize and find out if any money goes for things that we do not need or want.

Here is a short list of expenses that many people have. Put a check mark next to ones you have, then write down any expenses you have, that are not on the list.

- Necessities like food

- Clothes laundry dry-cleaning

- Car and transportation expenses: gas, oil, parking, license, plates, car repair, train fare or bus fare

- Rent, mortgage payments, heat, electricity, phone, water, property taxes, house repair, appliance and repair, furniture, small items for home, cleaning supplies on the yard care,

- Medical and dental expenses: doctor, dentist, drugs, hospital or clinic.

- Savings: short to medium term for something soon, a future purchase, emergencies, investments.

- Installment payments: car, furniture, appliances, charge accounts, credit card accounts, loans.

- Pocket money, personal allowances, tobacco, beer, wine and hair care.

- Entertainment, movies and eating out Recreation, sports and equipment, club membership, newspaper, magazines, cable TV, records and tapes, DVDs videos and other multimedia, vacation, letters and postage.

- School bills, books, room and board at school, workshops, special training courses, lessons, music and more.

- Donations: church or synagogue, charitable giving, charities, other and gifts

- Insurance: (if not deducted from your pay check): life, health, house, car and property

- Taxes: (if not deducted from your pay check): Federal, state and local income, social security

Which other ones could you list ?

- **Finding out how much you actually spend on each expense**

This is the hard part, where some thought and effort will have to go into the process to ensure the most accurate information is recorded. This will give a realistic and real-time estimate that is reliable and accurate.

In this section, you need to ask yourself how much each item on your list actually costs how much each item costs you a month.

The following estimates and guidelines could prove helpful to you as you set up your family budget:

- <u>Monthly bills that stay the same</u> – car and rental payments

- <u>Monthly bills that change</u> – utilities, phones and more. Find costs per month for say six months, add them up. Take this number you have calculated and divide it by six (the amount of months) to get your average cost. This is the number you will be using for your budgetary exercise.

- <u>Bills that come every three or six months</u> – the number for every month will be used in your budgetary process.

- <u>Bills that come annually, meaning once a year</u> – divide the amount by 12 months. The answer is your monthly budget number.

- <u>Bills that come more than once a month</u> – food, gas, lunch and family fun. This is a category to watch very closely, as it is a contributor to this "bottomless pit", we sometimes feel and see our cash disappear into.

- <u>Unexpected expenditures or surprise bills</u> – what you can afford to set aside as a buffer or emergency, contingency fund - (look at the last three years or so and see what kind of unexpected expenses you and your family faced). Use an estimate that makes sense to you and divide the annual number by twelve months to get your monthly number.

- **Finding out if monthly expenses match monthly take-home pay**

Compare your total expenses with your take-home pay. A couple of results and scenarios could be staring you in the face:

<u>Positive result:</u> Income more than expense – you can either spend or save!

<u>Negative result:</u> Expense more than income – spending more than you have, you might have to cut costs and try to save some money to cover the bases!

Whichever of these outcomes you are faced with, knowing is better than not knowing. For some this might bring little comfort and relief, but people in general, find this exercise useful to make an unknown more measurable. It makes us both accountable and wanting to act, faster and that sense of urgency and momentum is just what the family budget process needs!

- **Finding ways to balance your budget**

Earlier it was stated that a good budget would mean income would be equal to expenses. Having a small surplus is no guarantee by any means. You might need this to cover and unexpected rise in oil and gas prices or a larger grocery bill due to a party you are hosting at home.

This almost brings the concept home of a sliding scale, flexibility and discretionary buffer categories in budgets to absorb this give-and-take roller-coaster ride that is family budgeting.

The good news is whether you are in the red so to speak or just scraping by, managing to save nothing or maybe a little, or even a lot, this process will highlight areas where your attention is needed right away. It gives direction and purpose and assists families to formulate their spending plans, goals, re-visit their needs, dreams and goals.

Balancing the budget is no easy task. Here are a few steps that we can suggest to make your life a little easier:

- Find out how much you need to cut from your expenses
- Decide you can make cuts in your expenses and be detailed
- Re-balance your income and expenses after you've made these cuts

A word to the wise: Do not make cuts in your budget that you cannot live with in real life. It is extremely important to remain realistic and keep your real-time expenses and living realities in the forefront of your mind when you make these decisions.

If you're getting out of a situation where you are in debt and short of cash, you have to try to curb spending any way you can. Cutting those expenses are crucial, not only because you are over budget.

We mean that there might be other reasons, like adding a budget-line to your overall planning for your family vacation. Realistically, we cannot add and address new needs and goals before we have fulfilled our duty and responsibilities.

Cutting a little here and there will mostly do the trick – cancel that newspaper subscription for the papers that just land in the recycle box or garbage anyway. Do you need all the specialty channels and packages on your Cable TV options? Can you live with giving some up?

There is always the specter of rising prices and interest rates, inflation and more to cope with as well, so building preparedness for that into your budget is also a priority. Whatever we can do to cut our costs and expenditure will benefit our pocketbooks and family budgets immensely!

Cutting back on things you need the least is a good starting point if you are at a total loss as to what and how to give something up, add a new line into your budget or plan for the future or inevitabilities. You are well on your way in the family budgeting process. You are doing it, every step of the way. Consolidate and re-visit your budget often – it is a dynamic process and 'living' document or tools so to speak to help you keep your fingers on the pulse of your financial situation.

Another useful strategy is to set up a bill-paying plan and process that will protect your interest. When, how and how much you get paid will all influence your course of action. Creative and innovative allocation of your paycheck is the key.

If you get paid once a month, the amounts in your budget will have to be paid monthly as is.

If you get paid twice a month, divide each budget item by two.

If paid bi-weekly (as is mostly the practice these days), still divide the monthly amount by two – it will not be the exact amount to plan for, but a rough and close estimate. In the end better than nothing!

If you are paid weekly, divide each budget item into 4. Cash flow management will form a big part of your fiscal strategy, once you have put your budget pen to paper and mapped out the needs and requirements. Utilize your cash, checking and savings account (if applicable) to pay for expenses. Do not pay your bills with your credit card!

Keep track of all your discretionary spending. A financial diary for a week is always a good idea to scribble down in every time you withdraw money, pay for something or open your purse without thinking.

This will provide you with insights you did not have before on where the money actually goes. It will also carry within it, clues to adjust budget lines if actual cost is higher on certain items. Spending patterns and behaviors will emerge that might surprise or shock you!

Having some wriggle-room and discretionary spending is always motivation. The occasional treat and indulgence, special night out or other family activity is that more enjoyable, if you know you have worked hard to earn it and deserve a pat on the back for all your fiscal responsibility and discipline!

Always keep one eye on the future folks… budgets might need to change again and again for a variety of reasons. You can never feel you have "arrived" completely and that your budget is set in stone. Family and life often throws us a curve ball or two, banks, service providers, government and fate sometimes do too!

Changing budgets should not be a source of frustration for you; it actually shows you that your family budgeting process is actually working. It is a real-time pulse and mechanism to capture these changes, which will leave you prepared and informed, ready to act and respond appropriately. This impetus for change can come from different sources.

Here are some examples:

Change of income, goals, rising prices, goals reached, family growing, moving and or relocating to a new place, family getting smaller, new spending habits, change in lifestyle or unplanned expenses.

If you can stick with it and see it through a family budget can help you meet your goals, get and stay out of debt, pay your bills on time, every time, keep track of your spending, cut costs and stretch your dollar to the max!

HINTS, TIPS, TOOLS AND TRICKS FOR SETTING UP A FAMILY BUDGET

"Creating a budget" captures in its expression and meaning, both the excitement and the apprehension most of us feel when we have to face our financial situation and or lack of planning and accountability in that area.

Most businesses would fail if they ran like we manage our household incomes sometimes. This is not a natural thing for people to <u>want</u> to do. It falls into that 'I will if I really have no choice' kind of categories.

However, worth mentioning is that we spend most of our waking hours at work, earning the cash we need to get by and cover our living expenses. Then, we do not take the time to plan what to do with it. We just respond, spend and move on, spiraling, circling around, aimlessly and oblivious mostly about the state of our financial affairs.

This is obviously not true for some of us, for whom planning and organizing comes naturally and budgeting is like second nature and breathing, we just do not think about it, get it done and then barely spare it a second thought. Both these types of approaches can hurt us in the long run.

Our society has also become so fast-paced and focused on success, that we sometimes lose sight of the future perspective, enjoying life and what we do have. We cannot really focus on our own financials for lots of "excuses", sorry reasons we provide like: trouble slowing down, taking a step back and evaluating our financial situations or not knowing how to set up a family budget.

One of the first hints or tips we provide is advocating fiscal awareness. This means evaluating openly, freely and honestly where things are at today for your finances and household.

The whole purpose and goal of creating or setting up a family budget is to enlighten and alleviate money pressures. Utilizing a tool that can assist you in getting back onto the road to financial freedom, fiscal responsibility and financial, budgetary health, positive cash flow, with money to spare would be the ideal work-tool to grasp and grab! As the previous pages have shown the process in itself is not altogether that difficult.

You can certainly see how this real-time, 'dollar and expenditure tracker' can assist you to be agile and respond to market, family and monetary pressure, changes and crises. Continue to revise and update your budget as your needs, family and circumstances change.

Money is such a daily necessity and ever-present in our comings and goings. There is no escaping it. It is everywhere and needed anywhere and all over. We have different currencies, structures, procedures and all around the world, but in the end, it is the currency that makes the world go round, fueling the global economy.

Seen from that perspective, we often feel that taking control of our own finances and expenditures will not have much of an impact, as we are all at the mercy of the wheels and gear of a churning economical machine, with government and banking rules, regulations, trade and principles, ethics and decision-making that affects our quality of life. However, this is simply not the case!

Good money management skills in the household is crucial, not only for survival and good financial state of affairs, it teaches our children how we think handling money should be taken care of. They watch us so closely.

We model certain behaviors, spending patterns, discipline or maybe throwing all caution to the wind with credit card spending, debt and reminder notices all over the house, creditors calling, afraid to walk to the mailbox to remove the bills, and more.

What chance do our children have to end up entangled in that spiraling and vicious circle we spoke about earlier? Money in, money out?

How do we get to the point where family budgeting is a learning tool to help us teach our kids to work better with their funds? Whether through allowances, mutual savings goals, their own account or more, as parents we have an opportunity to instill some solid financial skills early on in life that will assist them later, as they work toward their independence and family budgets of their own!

Do some of your own soul-searching before you start your budgeting process. How motivated are you to plan, set-up and stick to a family budget? Would you do it now? Today? If you knew how?

Then let us get started, together. There are lots of practical suggestions for setting up a family or household budget. We will never be able to cover them or the mechanics and intricacies all here at once. You will however continue to find in these pages valuable insights and tit-bits to help you pursue better fiscal management and cash flow, budgeting in general.

It is all about making your dollar go further. Investing in the time and effort that it will take to get to that point of greater financial security and possibly even have a surplus eventually!

1: Take stock and face the facts head-on, honestly and with serious commitment, drive and purpose. Assessing your own capital worth and analyzing your home life and situation from a financial perspective is of utmost importance.

2: Plot your own course. Formulate some financial goals and lay out your own roadmap on how to get where you need and want to be financially speaking.

3: Take a thorough, critical and factual look at your fiscal situation and status. Unbiased and honest is best. Get a most recent credit report and look over your bank and credit cards statements, tax returns and other financial sources of information: stock portfolio, RRSP's and more.

Get a financial planner to assist you if you are unsure about what to use and include or not in this assessment. You might also want to take a broader perspective and discuss retirement, priorities, insurance needs, will and testament and more, because, like financials, we never seem to take these crucial life planning tasks and to do very seriously and barely give them second thought or time of day! The time is now and the place is here to take control of your financial situation and life.

4: Committing the time and effort to build your financial action and spending plan, budget and goals should get priority and might just be the most valuable undertaking and time well spent, not wasted you might ever set aside!

5: Think of how you define your own financial worth. Reflect on what it is, what you base it on. Is it concrete data and fact, perception or maybe even a wild guess or estimate? Income, savings and all of your other assets work together to give you the whole fiscal picture.

This side of the balance sheet for most people remains fixed and is relatively easy to do, when they put their minds to it.

6: Always remember that this process and document known as a family budget is only going to be as good as the data and updates you provide! When acquiring new assets, ensure that this side of the balance sheet is strengthened appropriately!

7: Adjust your focus slightly to more in-depth and longer term. We live so much in the moment, especially if we purchase things or spend our money. We just look at the cost today and do not think of interest over time and this being the total cost of course.

8: Actually setting financial goals will also energize you, give you a reason to work towards something meaningful. You might even start to enjoy uncovering opportunities for frugal choices, 'penny-pinching' and what we prefer to call creative savings techniques!

9: Become financially literate and master the family budget process, tools and worksheets, spending logs. Demystify some of the complexities and just try some fiscal responsibilities, without being overwhelmed by the intricacies of calculations and more.

Remember, there is always professional help out there, once you have gotten started, completed the grunt and groundwork to move in and on to a comprehensive consultation with a personal, professional financial planner, who can explain the lay of the land, impact of your situation and plan in more detail.

Most of them will offer the first consultation free to assess your situation for you. Most of them utilize state-of-the-art software and technology industry-related and customized tools that shed light on even the darkest situation, to find a little ray of hope and a couple of dollar at the end of the tunnel. There is a way out of the abyss.

10: Family budgeting can be used to teach you good fiscal habits: get in the habit of paying in cash, using your credit cards only for emergencies.

Learn how to stop buying on impulse and use your willpower to walk away, say no thank you and leave it at that. Shop at wholesale and discount department stores. Respect your budget limits and stick to it. Buy generic medicine and support your discount pharmacy.

Always try to find ways to supplement your income, part-time jobs, your own business or rent a room or floor in your house, offer storage, invest in real estate and take in a boarder or tenant.

Turn your thermostat way down in your house and turn off a few lights. Winterize your house from top to bottom. Eliminate and treat areas where heat and energy is lost. Cut back on home and cell phone use. Check insurance policies shop around and raise your deductible to lower your monthly bill.

In isolation, these probably do not have a lot of impact individually, but when they are combining in a well-planned, cleverly executed family budget, with discipline and consistency, they will start to make a difference and you will start to see the benefits and impact on your bottom line.

11: A family budget is a learning tool and process to empower individuals and families to better self-manage their financial resources, spending, cost cutting and household finances. In general You will be able to set-up your own personal or family budget.

By tackling the skill and mastery of smart budgeting, you will have a greater understanding eventually of <u>exactly where</u> and <u>by how much</u>, you need to **adjust expenses to either live within your means** or **know how much extra you need to maintain your current lifestyle**.

12: Other family budgeting process steps will require you to be able to identify and categorize all your expenses and, coupled with an easy to set-up and follow filing system, create the backdrop and framework for all future budgeting and fiscal planning at home or elsewhere.

13: Family budgeting is not something that is taught by parents or schools; however it is such a simplistic concept, process and task that it is almost unthinkable that we are not placing greater focus on it these days.

In the end, it is all about what you <u>DO,</u> to make ends meet, which implies action. To be in charge of your finances; family budgeting gives you a sense of real understanding and control over your money, not the other way around. Money is a 'tool' and life necessity but it does not prescribe how you should live or spend it.

14: Family budgets allow you to gain knowledge you would otherwise not have had at your fingertips, concerning your own and family finances.

For example: Knowing where and what expenses you can affect or effectively change, to cut costs appropriately, timely and immediately in certain cases is very helpful.

15: To enable your family budgeting process set up an easy and orderly log, record-keeping and filing system; and make spending notes often to track your money and habits. Trust me, we do not know where all our money goes. We are just certain of one thing and that it slips through out fingers, hands and pockets, cards and plastic, fast!

16: Understanding, explaining and sharing the benefits of good budgeting with others is pivotal, to get them on-board and participating actively in the family budgeting process. Ask for their ideas and input. Two heads are better than one in most cases. They might think of savings opportunity, consolidations and or things to do without, that you did not even think about or considered for a second!

17: Here are some more family budgeting summary steps to remember:

- Identify and categorize all expenses – look at categories and line items, types and timing of expenses, amounts and budget accordingly. Remember categories like miscellaneous, discretionary, maintenance, emergency and others. These will also provide you with a little more flexibility when you do have to massage your money, budget and cash flow processes to meet need, demands and change.

- It is of utmost importance that we are able as family budgeters to allocate and adjust expense items, prioritize need with foresight, discretion, informed choice and empowered confidence, stemming from core and in-depth knowledge and accurate information.

- Practice utilizing a basic budgeting framework and recording method in your family budgeting and formulate your very own personal and or simple 'Home Budget' or rough first draft of your financial situation – a kind of YOU ARE HERE situational analysis. Chances are you will see and learn something you did not know before.

- Even if you feel you just have a basic understanding of budgeting and how it can improve your own management of your own and household finances will make a difference. Take the time out to explore and try putting your first one together, following the steps given earlier in this booklet.

This guide and its content, will appeal to almost anybody:
- anyone who recognizes the need to budget;
- those who have never or not yet learnt how to budget;
- individuals or groups who are looking for a first-step debt-consolidation strategy and technique,
- someone who has come into some money through a lottery, casino win, gift or inheritance and want to ensure they know how to budget properly before they start spending left, right and centre.
- It is good for moms , dads, grandparents, children, friends and families to do.
- It fosters independence and fiscal responsibility, accountability and stewardship.
- Even those with reasonable income, now receiving less, will find some answers here.
- The one who needs to understand expenses that need to be adjusted; and
- even those who prefer to feel and be in control of their expenses.

- Family budgeting enables them to be in the position to know where they need to modify their lifestyle and make significant adjustments to ensure a bright and happy financial future.

Some of the most important process elements and content pieces of family budgeting to read more about, study, learn and practice, hone and refine are:

- A fundamental understanding of the principles, merits and mechanics of budgeting and the budgeting process itself. All the process steps to get your through the journey and to the resulting document, tool or magic numbers!
- Distinguish between fixed, variable and discretional expenditure(s)
- Identify and categorize all expenses, breaking them into categories and line items, time-frames, other detailed sub-classifications and clustering;
- How to set-up housekeeping budgets and what to consider
- Identifying hidden expenses
- Identifying areas of discretionary spending, habits and perhaps over-spending risk areas
- Setting up expenditure recording systems
- Decide on the best way suitable for you and your family to monitor what you spend
- Set-up a very basic Home/Personal Budget Filing System
- Any calculations, formulas and budget principles you think will help you maximize and optimize your cash flow and money-management

Another great way to learn about family budgeting is to ask around and to learn from others. With the internet at our disposal, there are numerous reliable sources of practical, tried, tested and true tips, strategies and techniques to follow. We selected but a few to provide a sample. Never underestimate the power of a shared experience!

Sometimes exploring a financial activity like family budgeting conceptually is not enough. Getting a practical perspective, with some hands-on tips can be more meaningful that a close description or analysis.

There are lots of definitions, opinions and numerous books have been written on the subject of budgeting for families, by families and others. In our information-age, knowledge is power these days and lots of parents and professionals share and voice their opinions openly on the internet, sharing and growing the body of knowledge. We selected a few examples to encourage others to explore these at their leisure as well.

Here are ELEVEN more practical suggestions and tips from online users posted on the internet on family budgeting:

1. Keep a record book as well as your bankbook
It takes time and requires a lot of self-discipline. Start each month with the balance and enter every payment, etc in advance, in the form of a calendar. It works well for most people due to the fact that they always have their actual working balance handy. Remember the comment about having your financial information at your fingertips? Here is a sure-fire way to get you on that path quickly.

2. Calendar Calculations
Putting regular bills on a calendar based on due dates and when salaries are received proves helpful to some. This helps specifically to get everything paid on time and keep in perspective where the money actually goes, since all miscellaneous expenses are also recorded.

3. Getting bills paid
Working out all the major and large bills (i.e., rent, car payment, insurance, etc.), dividing it up so every week, that amount is removed from the family 'paycheck'. Therefore, at the end of the month, there is need or risk to lose an entire paycheck to rent or car registration.

4. 1-2-3-4 Plan
Divide all bills weekly. A set amount goes to a savings account each week. When there is a 5th Friday in a month, you have a "free paycheck" to save.

5. Open a household account
In a second checking account, deposit a sum that covers your monthly expenses. Have all of your bills automatically withdrawn. This account acts as a holding cell for household obligations - the primary account is for day-to-day operations. Works for me!

6. A timely budget

Get a notebook. List expenses and their due dates. Divide payments into small amounts & use labeled envelopes for payments and money storage. Reduce duplicate credit usage to 1 or 2 credit cards. Use the net for bill paying and to check your accounts.

7. Yearly savings

Making a list of all annual or once-a-year type bills (car registration, shots for pets, school pictures, etc.) and divide them by 12. Save this amount each month and, when one of these items come up, you have the money to pay it. No more surprises.

8. Save credit card receipts

Keep an envelope in the car for the credit cards you use. When you buy anything using a card, put the receipt in the envelope as soon as you enter the car. Keep changing the envelope every month. This will save you time and hassle when looking for receipts.

9. Only twice a month

Separate all bills to be paid on either the 1st or 15th of the month. This enables you to pay all bills at once and on time. An added bonus is that you will also immediately know how much money you have left over for entertainment, vacation and other discretionary items.

10. Split into Savings and Checking

Figure out a budget based on a savings account/checking account split. Savings builds up for things like real estate taxes, vacations, and insurance. Checking is monthly (e.g. phone, groceries, etc.). Split your monthly income into the savings and checking accounts according to the budget. Savings amounts are strictly budgeted. The checking account is controlled by watching the balance until the next payday.

11. Respect your partners need for financial security

Everyone likes to buy their toys, but the overall financial security of the household needs to be considered first. I am not against toys; just save up the money first to buy them versus putting non-essential day-to-day expenses on credit.

An example of a toy in my relationship was the spouse's need to have a big expensive truck in the driveway. I was not against the truck, I was against the debt to purchase the truck when there was no money in the savings or money built up for college tuition. Be considerate of the overall family financial situation and provide financial security for your family.

Moreover, on 'living within a family budget', online users listed FOURTEEN more great practical suggestions on family budgeting:

1. Stay busy after work

One "easy" way to avoid overspending and thus stay within your budget is to have something else to do after work. Get a second job that is fun, go to school, volunteer or get into great physical shape. The more you do, the less you will spend!

2. Watch those miscellaneous categories

Make sure you have enough well-defined categories to capture your true spending. Putting too much into a miscellaneous category makes it harder to track what you have spent and harder to control, especially the splurges!

3. Need

If you did not know you need it, you probably do not. Do not buy things just because they are on sale. If you had no use or want for it before you saw it on sale, then you will have no use for it later.

4. Save money for special occasions on a budget

Add up how much you will spend on Christmas, birthdays, etc. Treat that total like it was a debt and make payments to a savings account for special occasions. Be sure to select a specific day of the month that your payment is due and stick with an amount.

5. Don't Forget to Budget for Special Occasions

When forecasting your expenses, remember to include gift-giving occasions. Mother's Day, Valentine's Day, birthdays, Christmas, and anniversaries are good examples. If you plan to spend money on these occasions, remember to include this in your budget.

6. Don't use a debt to get out of another debt

Do not take out a consolidation loan to pay off your other debts. The point is to get out of it, not to squeeze them together and end up paying interest on the loan while paying off your debts. Try consulting a "free" debt counselor service first.

7. Remember To Budget Time As Well

We have all heard "time is money." Well-spent time can be an investment. Take a few minutes to plan ways to save on bills - 15 or 20 min. researching lower rates on electricity or long distance can pay off. You will know when time spent is not worth it.

8. The envelope system

Total yearly/monthly bills, divide each into 12 months. Divide monthly amount into bi-weekly payments. Use envelope for each bill; put in cash every 2 weeks. Use only the cash in envelope till it is gone. Do not touch your account/debt card! Envelopes ONLY!

9. Good teeth cheaper

You can go to a dental school to have your teeth cleaned, filled, orthodontic work done, etc. The cost is approximately half what you would usually pay. Note: Make sure you have some extra time as this takes a little longer.

10. Avoid expensive friends

Avoid friends who want to go for drinks all the time or suggest an evening at home. The money you spend on drinks and snacks, can buy something better, or go into your savings account. Also avoid friends who want to have supper at your house because you are a "good cook" what that really means is that they are saving money while you are grocery shopping.

11. Keep Track of Your Expenses on a Daily Basis

I call the bank's automated line and do my banking every single night before I go to bed. I can see what checks and/or debits from my debit card are posted and what my running balance is. I compare with what I have in my checkbook or with receipts. This only takes about 10 minutes. Often people get into trouble when they try to keep a running total of what they have left in their head and get into trouble.

12. How To Live Within Your Budget

Organize, budget, and beat stress.

13. Know what you spend

Establishing a budget, and periodically entering all of your purchases into money managing software, should take the guesswork out of your finances. At the beginning, minor changes will most likely need to be made to your budget. Once you have a finalized budget, one person should be responsible for maintaining the budget and tracking finances. I sit down with my wife on a monthly basis and go over our financial results. If we are close to exceeding a budget line item during the month, I will tell my wife and we adjust our spending accordingly.

14. Cut down on interest

With bills happening throughout the month, people can find themselves poor one part of the month, and rich during the other. My bank offers free online bill pay, so I take all of my bills, and divide it by 4. I then pay weekly, so I always have the same spending cash each pay check. It also cuts down on the interest that accrues.

Sometimes, just listening to the opinions of others opens up our minds to other possibilities we have not thought of, read about or seen in any published material, industry-related text-books or budget specialist tip sheets and 'how to' layouts. All the technical information, procedural and budgeting principles are extremely important if you want to ensure lasting and sustainable change. It is also undeniably true, that in this day and age, collaborating and connecting with others is how we learn.

Utilizing online sources, electronic publications and shared experiences, solving common problems together is definitely the wave of the future. Some providers online offer 'live' customer consultations.

These are mainly for financial issues and mostly your first hour is free. If you are in a real crunch, crises and need a budget fast, but do not have the time to even read through the Coles-notes version, then maybe the internet has the answer for you. Always remember that you are the best-informed and decision maker in this process.

Taking control of your finances should challenge, invigorate and excite you. You are taking charge of your life, getting your ducks in a row so to speak and traveling down the road of fiscal responsibility and re-connection.

It is mostly a money crunch or crisis situation that make us lean towards budgeting more. Handling a money crisis well and realizing that family budgeting is but one pieces of that puzzle, might be helpful. The expectations, problems faced, context and depth of the crisis, is as important as the steps, procedures, techniques, tools and budget worksheets you end up using.

- Admitting that there is a problem is normally considered a good first step. Asking for help is a close second. Money-matters makes us do strange things. You are probably not the only one facing this situation. Therefore, take heart there is help out there. Even before getting to the how to steps for your own budget, work on your state of mind, immediate needs, concerns, dues and crisis. Consult a professional financial planner, who will assist you, in all likelihood, through and financial analysis of your situation, assembling facts and information, coming up with solutions, suggestions and alternatives you probably are not thinking of right now. Even when not under pressure or in crisis, when setting up a family budget, gather your thought, emotions, data, receipts, statements, input from others, discuss, consult, assemble, synergize and prepare to succeed. Get the most appropriate, accurate information you possibly can before setting up any expense categories or filling out worksheets. Get and extra set of eyes to look it over, you will not regret it.

- Sober, even-keel, un-emotional, rational, clear-minded, level-headed and ready to take on any challenge – include setting up a personal and family budget, income, expense statements, asset-liability summaries, expense categories, line items, amounts, estimates and more. Committed to succeed, with a positive attitude and financial resourcefulness will serve you well in any situation, no matter what the money crunch or reason for your budgeting need may possibly be.

- Take responsibility and have realistic expectations.

- Take some risks when required. Be pro-active and explore your options. Do not hesitate to tackle controversial topics or expenditures, even if it can lead to conflict and disagreement. Couples and finances have always caused some difficulty, so it is all normal. Stabilize your situation, salvage what you can and move on, focus forward. Family budgeting has the past, present, future continuum all covered.

- Someone suggested that there are eleven steps in any new money management endeavor you undertake where personal interest and stake is high:

Step One	Change Your Expectations and be Realistic
Step Two	Tell Yourself the Truth – Face the Music
Step Three	Decide How to Pay for Necessities – Stop-gap Solutions
Step Four	Identify Your Assets – all of them! They are there, we just need to go find them
Step Five	Discover How Much You Cost – this is how much you spend and your contribution to situation and circumstance
Step Six	Calculate What You Can Afford to Cost – cost cutting and balancing your budget
Step Seven	Call Your Creditors – dealing with debt
Step Eight	Quit Paying Late Fees – work with professionals
Step Nine	**Create a Family Budget**
Step Ten	Do Not Ignore the Following: IRS, Parking tickets, Association Fees, Car payment, Immigration and other government affiliates that need to be pulled into your situation to assist you as best they can

It is no surprise then, to even find the ever-popular 'budgeting' concept among these listed must do's to re-collect, re-orient and return to fiscal freedom and avert further money-related crises!

HOW SHOULD A FAMILY BUDGET BE USED

This question immediately suggests that it should be part of the whole family budgeting process. It is much part of the learning around setting it up, considering its usefulness, function and purpose.

Creating or setting up the budget is one thing. Sticking to it, effectively implementing, sustaining and if actual fact, in essence 'using' it is the ultimate goal and achievement. That is worth celebrating. Families have different ways again to use or refer to their family budgets.

For some it will be no more than a general guideline. For others it would constitute an absolute rule not to be bent or broken. Others still will use the family budget as a strategic planning tool to protect the interests of his/her family and plan for a full and happy life, setting a small amount aside for the future, invested smartly and securely, with confidence and pride.

The very day the family budget actually assists you in reducing your spending and making informed smart financial decisions that is the day you do not sit back and relax, but throw all your energy back in making it even better. This is an on-going, continuous improvement exercise, experiment and undertaking of your own making, design and creation!

The family budget can:

- **Assist you in handling unforeseen increases in costs and unbudgeted expenses**

It is very common to get discouraged when on the family budgeting path. The minute you feel you have taken strides forward, something will happen, a setback, unexpected upset or expense, breakdown, maintenance or replacement or car, appliance, major purchase or repair and many other setbacks will occur.

In a sense it makes families more robust, responsive and adaptable. Tracking your finances makes you aware of patterns and business cycles, cost and many other factors that affect hearth and home financial life and health. Rent increases, more expensive cigarettes or tax increases, higher gas or energy prices or increased mileage to and from work are but a few examples of these events and issues that might come up.

When faced with these challenges, problems or complexities, having your fingers on the pulse of your available resources, discretionary monies, savings, line of credit, rates, banking fees and more, will all help you make the right informed decision that is best for your family, at that time and act accordingly with diligence and confidence. You are in control of your financial situation and not the other way around. It enlightens and empowers you to do more with less!

Unpredictable pricing and fluctuating expense are not easy to reduce in any budget. Having this variation handy, spread over a period of time, can help you plan better and anticipate sudden spikes or higher expenditure during certain months of the year.

For example, the telephone bill is higher when the teenagers are home for the summer. Emergency, contingency and improvements are not priorities for most of us when we receive our paycheck. To ensure a steady stream of income into these categories make "saving for a rainy day" come to life and have some real impact and meaning in our financial planning.

Cutting non-essentials first is a good strategy. Alcohol, long distance phone calls, gifts, gardening and landscaping services, decorating costs, pet care needs, recreation and lottery tickets can all be good money-saving categories. The more line items you can include, in your cost reduction, the smaller the dollar-amount impact in each.

It should come as not surprise that by just cutting a little in each of these categories, families can easily save upwards of $240 per year without too much noticeable difference in their lifestyle or any major disruptions or sacrifices. If is less than1 % of your total spending, it should not really cause pain, grief or reason for worry.

Family budgets can also provide hints on how to save on non-essentials: Buying more or less of a product or service, comparison shopping for the lowers possible price, bulk and discount, sale, buying a lower-priced or no-name brand. Eliminating some gift giving (Christmas, birthdays, friends and family) is a way to save money.

Elimination of waste is another clever way to save money that is often overlooked, BUT not in the family budget. Thrown out food because too much was purchased or it spoils because at time of purchase it was not as fresh as it could have been. Spur-of-the-moment clothing purchases, too trendy, uncomfortable and not the right size perhaps?

Making an active effort to participate in the family budgeting process will carry its own rewards as well. Self-discipline and curbing your own spending will soon become second nature almost.

- **Enable families to make large spending reductions in the right places at the appropriate times**

Anything from a small rent increase of a couple of dollars to an all-out job-loss can impact home life and finances, and not in a positive sense. The family budget offers you the opportunity to prepare somewhat for this, whether pro-active or responsive action follow. Flexibility and adaptability are bonuses with family budgeting.

It will spell out the reality, damage, impact, what needs to be done at the barest of minimums to get by and offer stop-gap solutions, practical and accessible, right away. It is not to say that it will have you not worrying about it! All of us will be concerned if this is our situation, but it will leave you more prepared to deals with the challenges head on and right away as opposed to wasting time wondering what to do and how bad it is.

- **Protect against income reduction and inevitabilities**

In the case of job loss mentioned above there are also immediate realities to consider. Financial implications are huge for family life and the pressure is on. Family budgets and informed budgeted will tell you that this tool and time spent will be worth every penny if this were ever to happen to them.

Because of the heightened awareness and familiarity with the context and content of the financial, spending and cost cutting plans and strategies, goals and savings, the family budget process and product now offer avenues to solutions rather than barriers of debt and no point of return.

Tackling normal spending categories first, reduced transportation costs, packing a lunch as opposed to having it in the cafeteria every day. Suspend all discretionary funding, move money in your accounts around to ensure liquid assets to cover basic expenses. Luxury items and recreation, sports and other leisure activities will be another category to find some budget dollars.

Maintenance and repair costs might be suspended or delayed, cost-cutting is never pleasant but the budgeting process makes it easier to know where the cushions and 'fat' is that can be trimmed or eaten away at, without risking heart and limb!

Other positive job-changes like promotions and relocations could also have a lot of impact. Taxes, relocation fees, buy-and-sell of homes, settling allowances, insurance, storage etc. they all add up. The family budget will help you assess your situation more clearly, leading to better decision-making and informed empowered choice.

Any discussion on 'How to set up a family budget', will be incomplete without a section dealing with debt and debt consolidation

Normally we use credit cards for a variety of good reasons, like convenience, business expenses, online commerce, instant accountability, unexpected bargains or expenses, medical and or other emergencies.

There are however, also very definite situations where plunging yourself deeper into debt is not a good idea at all:

- An expensive item you know you cannot afford (indulgence shopping). If you do not have the cash funds to purchase it, charging it is not going to make it easier for you to pay it! By putting it on plastic you just racked up the price and interest charges. Your budget will not thank you later for this one. Bad decisions often lead us down the wrong path. You will be left facing paying for this choice for a couple of years down the road still.
- Tele shopping or infomercials for gadgets and widgets.
- When grocery shopping, pay cash rather than plastic, or you will most likely overspend.
- Meals, drinks, nights out and other entertainment charges are all like the miscellaneous category in a budget. The balance and dues will just keep on piling up, if it is not tracked and monitored closely
- If you are truly going to be budget-minded and money conscious while trying to get out of debt, consolidating or in debt-repair avoid the plastic!

- Check the interest rates on your card, consolidate accounts, go through the exercise of balance transfers et al. and seek the advise of a professional to assist and advise you, on how best to approach credit of any sort while on the mend to financial freedom, reputation, repair and recovery.
- For family budgeting purposes, credit cards are for EMERGENCIES ONLY and should not be used to pay for bills or luxury items. Carrying a high balance, missing a payment, paying less than the minimum or other faux pas, might negatively affect your credit rating and undermine all the other good work you were doing in your budgeting process.
- Watch out for steeper late charges, higher rates, annual service fees, interest rates and charges, and cash advances.
- Using your credit card at an ATM for a cash advance can sometimes not be convenient, as the rate and cash advance fees can total as much as 24% or higher. This is even more than loan sharks or other payday like loan providers.
- Do not use credit cards for any of the following reasons: unbudgeted expenses you cannot pay for; having no cash savings to help you with unexpected expenses, consuming more than you can afford or impulse shopping.

Debt management and family budgeting actually fit like hand-in-glove together. They compliment and strengthen each other if used appropriately and with caution, diligence and commitment to change.

It is advisable to get a handle very early on in your budgeting process on what exactly the debt situation is. For most people this is the most painful part of the process. Facing their monetary past and the aftermath of overspending, lack of budgeting and large debt!

Extreme care should be taken early on as well to protect your financial interest. Review your family budget spending categories and avoid debt by every means you can and not use it for living expenses.

Repaying your debt should be the main priority. Consulting with a financial planning and debt consolidation professional and specialist will help you answer the question whether you need to consolidate, transfer, stop using credit cards all together, file for bankruptcy or what your other options are. Exhaust all the possibilities before pursuing this route.

A personal debt review can be painful, but is very necessary to assess the status quo or where you are now and how good or bad it is. What is the depth of your "obligation" category in your budget, where this will inevitably fall.

Debt is a wide concept, covering lots of things, including mortgage, car, credit cards and other retail credit card accounts and personal loans of any kind. IOU's from family or friends also have to be included, if you are honest about making a difference, repaying in a timely fashion and truly want to know how bad it really is!

Your summary sheet can carry the following headings: account, total amount due, monthly payment, total interest paid last year, and interest rate. Financial advisors call this a debt review register. It is painful to see this data, because it will clearly show the impact of bad financial decision-making. Interest paid gives you absolutely NO BENEFIT WHATSOEVER!

Strategies for debt and cash flow management in a family budget include:
- Consolidating all consumer debt (that is everything you owe, except for your mortgage) and making it a priority to pay it off in a timely fashion, getting reduced rates and maximizing your effort in wiping the financial slate clean.
- Paying off high-interest credit cards first
- Use a line of credit if you can as the interest rates are typically lower
- Suspend any kind of spending on any credit card and establish good habits paying in cash for purchases
- Use all store-based cards wisely or not at all, if that is the disciplined approach you have chosen
- Store-based card often have no annual fees and you could qualify for them even with a low credit score – showing restraint and good fiscal management by making your payments on time, every time and keeping the account up to date, will go a long way to regaining your confidence and repairing your credit.
- Utilize the service of a good credit counseling service to assist you and deal with your habitual over-spending and shopping addiction
- Use credit card statements for budgeting purposes for accuracy and tracking
- Loans are handled no differently – the strategy is pretty much the same: find the highest loan balance and the highest rate and start paying the latter first
- Avoid any new debt

- If after a six month period you have paid like clockwork, contact your creditors and negotiate a lower rate at that time to ease the burden a little bit
- Student and educational loans are approached as investments in your future and is a hybrid and shoulder debt category really. Loan-payback for all tuition debt needs to be included in your family budget. Taking a second job (evenings and weekends might be the answer here, ,while honing and practicing your skills and gaining some more experience as well!). This might lead to better business opportunity later and higher paying jobs later in life!

Take heart. Family budgets are not here to depress you even further. The fact that you are taking pro-active measures to participate in your life, ,sends the right signals, not only to creditors and credit counselors, but also to the family members that care so deeply about you too!

Another popular topic for family budgets, is children and fun activities. How to make the most of these togetherness opportunities, while living and functioning within limited means and on a budget, causes many money wise parents concern:

- "The best things in life are FREE" – you just need to know where to find them, how to look and then enjoy them together. Being cash-strapped or budget-challenged should not minimize the FUN you as a family have together.
- Prioritize it together with the other members and the children in the home (if they are older), discussing alternatives like picnics, walks, visiting a beach, lake or park close-by.
- Look for locations with lots of open-area space, baseball fields, tennis courts, and basketball courts.
- Use coupons for entertainment like DVD rentals, miniature golf and other sports.
- Matinee rates for movies are a great way to save money.
- Play board games with friends, arrange potlucks and play-dates.
- Visit zoos and museums and outdoor summer concerts that are usually free of charge.
- Add fun elements to choosing, like putting the activities in a hat and letting other choose what to do next.
- Avoid window shopping, mall-crawling or expensive shops where you will be tempted to spend more money or leave feeling guilty that you cannot.
- For discounted, bargain-priced brand-name kids clothing, shopping at end of season sales is a real budgetary blessing!

- Budget for one very special outing or event, you can do as a family and set aside a little extra if you can for that annual camping, local or road trip you plan for, in your family budgeting process each and every year.

Family budgets is not all doom and gloom. There are always ways to do little things together, make memories and invest time and attention in one another that costs absolutely nothing but time, a smile, a hug or two and a caring heart to share them all with!

FINAL THOUGHTS ON SETTING UP A FAMILY BUDGET

- **None of us want to remain or be without money, short on cash, cash-strapped and not able to live well and or get the things we need, dream about and want.** Family budgeting brings us one-step closer to our fiscal realities, while offering more than the direction and route, but also the tools and techniques to get to fiscal nirvana!

- **Most of us have an inherent want to protect what is rightfully ours**. Our hard-earned cash is no exception here. We want to enable, as far as it is in our power, to utilize what little (or much) we do have to the best advantage and our family benefit overall. Family budgeting helps us do so with method, structure, elements and processes that enable success.

- **Family budgeting can assist have and have nots alike make better financial decisions with a future perspective always in mind.**

- **Building greater awareness of where our money actually goes, or ends up, can be enlightening and empowering at the same time**. Some react with shock and horror, as they realize they are their own worst enemy. They bear witness to impulse-driven shopping and periods with no fiscal discipline. Realizing that this course of action hurt you and your family in the long run, puts a sudden halt on the money flowing out typically! (even if the effect does not last too long!)

- Although family budgeting can be overwhelming at first, the tools and techniques, process and steps to follow are fairly simple, straightforward and easy. Like so often said, it is not rocket science! We just need to have the right attitude, motivation and persistence to see and follow things through. Budget or bust!

- Family budgeting can help you get, be and remain in control of your money and family's financial situation. Be kind to your pocketbook!

- Set aside time to work on your household financials and budgeting processes on a regular basis. Keep it up to date and accurate. This way you can spot problems early, react quickly and come up with creative solutions in the short-term to address any issues, challenges or shortfalls. Be on top of things.

- Family budgeting helps you know your own financial facts. You will be able to know, instinctively and exactly what is going on with your cash-balance without even looking at your statement necessarily! A good test to tell whether someone is using a family budget for their household is to have them write down the exact amount they have in the bank today, and as of now also on their person, in their wallet. Add the two and write down the total right now.

What did you learn from this exercise? Let us take it one-step further. What do you owe? Include credit cards, car financing, mortgage and other debt. Subtract what you owe from what you have. Have you learnt anything by doing this simple exercise? For most of us the answers would be astonishing! This hands-on involvement and knowledge about your finances helps some and not others. For some of us just glancing at our statement now and again, having no idea as to what is in our wallets, is quite all-right too. (That is, as long as you are not finding ways to spend it without realizing it!)

- In family budgeting, do not be hesitant to set stretch-goals too. Whether you get there by cost cutting, taking a second, part-time or seasonal job or find another source of supplemental income, it helps your raise the bar even higher.

- Family budgeting is not just about budgeting to the last cent and flying by the seat of your pants. It offers structure, wisdom, decision making and reward for the serious and tenacious amongst us. Taking it on as a major and regular task and priority will change your quality of life, sometimes without you even realizing it.

- You are in it for the long haul! Take responsibility for spending. It this means laying down some ground-rules in your household and cutting back on a couple of luxury items, that needs to be discussed, agreed upon and stuck to, to make your budget work and have an impact over time.

- Family budgeting is about minimizing and totally avoiding if possible any unexpected and deemed unnecessary spending. Spell out the realities and consequences of these purchases to others – short on cash, family tension, unnecessary stress and complications, hardship and more. Openly discussing it builds fiscal responsibilities on all fronts. This does not mean rigidity or inflexibility. Need, merit, means and circumstance will obviously dictate.

- Family budgeting is also about shared responsibility. All members can participate – even the kids. Taking responsibility for the grocery bill for example. Mom is responsible mainly for the weekly outing to the store, but when it comes to the staples like milk, bread, eggs and cheese, one of the teenagers can be entrusted with the budget funds and task, help shop for bargain, check flyers and more. Setting house-rules about who gets to pay for what and when is also important when you have young adults still living in the house or have boarders. Family budgeting allows the channel for discussion and eventually mutual agreement on financial goals and priorities.

- Perhaps the most important part of all, is that family budgeting helps us all learn where the money actually goes, as opposed to where we think it does or should go. Normally very different things! The initial realization of the amounts (usually larger than we think!), involved on incidental, discretionary and impulse buying is an eye-opener for most and ends up saving families all kinds of money they never knew they had. Just brining that into the awareness and our conscious mind tends to put a stop to unnecessary expenditure.

- Mall crawling and hanging out in retail stores to kill time, is counter-productive and part of the reason we spend frivolously. From bookstores, to lottery tickets, gourmet coffee, food-court lunch, and a quick movie, items you do not really need, but think you or your spouse or kids would like leads to hasty, flawed and almost distorted decision making. The thought, actions and actually purchases are not budget-driven and money conscious at all. All these things add up over time. Smoking, daily coffee (or two), buying candy, chocolates, pop, magazines and more to 'kill time' are all money-guzzlers that should be avoided.

- Other examples of incidental money-guzzlers are parking meters, donuts, shoe repair, ,raffle tickets, fund-raising, car wash, pay phone. Avoid it is probably unrealistic, but family budgeting, logging and tracking at least makes us more aware of these categories and 'traps'. Have a category in your budget for Miscellaneous and track it for say 3-6-12 months and see how it adds up!

- Beware the flyers, advertisements, special discounted sales and other retail or sales tricks of the trade that tempt, entice and lure you in to spend your precious dough!

- Keep on tracking spending and income no matter what. A good tip for family budgeting is, at least initially, get a notebook and a pen and write things down as opposed to going to high-tech, spending money to get it done etc. Avoid this being or becoming just another unexpected and unplanned expense! It is supposed to help you, not hurt you. Tools are great, but process and results are better.

- Family budgeting help you focus on the different types of expense you and your family and household face. The annual ones are the hardest, we tend to put them on the back burner and they tend to be larger amounts too. Having them in your budget assist us not forgetting there major expenses like school fees, judo or gym memberships, dance classes, Christmas and birthday gifts, babysitting or nanny-salaries and more.

- Fiscal restraint, wise decisions, weighing options, informed choice, planned set and formulated goals and projection estimates and steps to get there, all work together in the family budget, to get you back on track and on the road to enjoying your dollar-earnings.

- Initially, when setting up your family budget probably for the first time, it is acceptable when estimating some of the expenditures and cost to err on the higher side. This will definitely show you where you would need to cut back if you had to add in budget line items or budget for big purchases like appliances, furnace replacement etc.

- Family budgets keep it real, in the moment and us humble, on our toes and accountable.

- Some realities we will have to live with. Some fixed costs we are not able to reduce right away or at all. The fact of the matter is, we are on the look-out and actively finding other and innovative ways to cut spending and costs that we would otherwise not have been motivated enough to do of our own accord.

- Surely, the most interesting effect of the family budget on most people, is revealing our personal spending habits, preferences, weaknesses or "buttons to push" my kids call them. Family budgeting helps us to get to know what they are and improve on them.

Where and why, on what and how much are all factors that impact while our money keeps vanishing. We are most often the biggest culprits here. Shopping excursions should be minimized; they are just a good excuse for buying unnecessary items.

Overspending while with a group of friends or peers are all too common these days. Grocery bills hide a lot of "sins" or impulse buying (chocolates, chips, magazines, ice cream etc.). Also knowing when during the year you tend to spend more money, is also important – bulk buying might be the answer. Think juice and snacks when the kids are home for summer for example. This also helps people realize that funds should be available almost year-round and that life is unpredictable.

- Family budgeting is one of those activities that none of us really truly value, until we see or feel it make a difference. If you stick with it long enough, disciplined and committed, you will experience the dynamic impact and life-altering influence and contribution of this tool and process. Happy number crunching! Have fun creating your own family budget.

Therefore, for now, we will stop our discussion here. Throughout these pages, attempts were made to show the need, benefits, nature, elements, advantages, processes and techniques for family budgeting that can get you started right away, offering practical advice and poignant suggestions that apply to your unique situation, whatever that may be.

We trust it has been time well spent and happy trails on your journey back to fiscal control, independence and empowered decision-making. PASS IT ON.

Some final thoughts, money saving perspectives and inspirations:

"If saving money is wrong, I don't want to be right!"　　　**William Shatner**
(Canadian Actor, Writer and Producer most famous for starring Captain Kirk in the television series Star Trek. b.1931)

"A simple fact that is hard to learn is that the time to save money is when you have some."
　　　　　　　　　　　　　　　　　　　　　　　　　　Joe Moore

"Save a little money each month and at the end of the year you'll be surprised at how little you have"
　　　　　　　　　　　　　　　　　　　　　　　　　Ernest Haskins

www.ingramcontent.com/pod-product-compliance
Lightning Source LLC
Chambersburg PA
CBHW050812180526
45159CB00004B/1633